My Name is Jacob

A Collection of Stories about People who Share my Name

By Allison Dearstyne

Dedicated to every boy named Jacob; may you take life by the horns and seize the day!

The name Jacob comes from the name Ya'qob in the Hebrew language. Translated to Latin, the name became Iacobus, which became Jacob when translated to English. Your name means "supplanter" or "he grabs the heel."

In the Torah and the Bible there is a story about baby Jacob grabbing his older twin brother Esau's heel as they were born. Later Jacob tricked Esau into trading his inheritance for a dinner. A supplanter is someone who takes the place of another person who was there first, just like Jacob in the Torah and the Bible.

Here are seven remarkable men named Jacob who changed their world, just like you will:

Jacob Lawrence
Jacob Riis
Jacob Grimm
Jacob Berzelius
Jacob Francis
Jakob Dylan
Jacob Bronowski

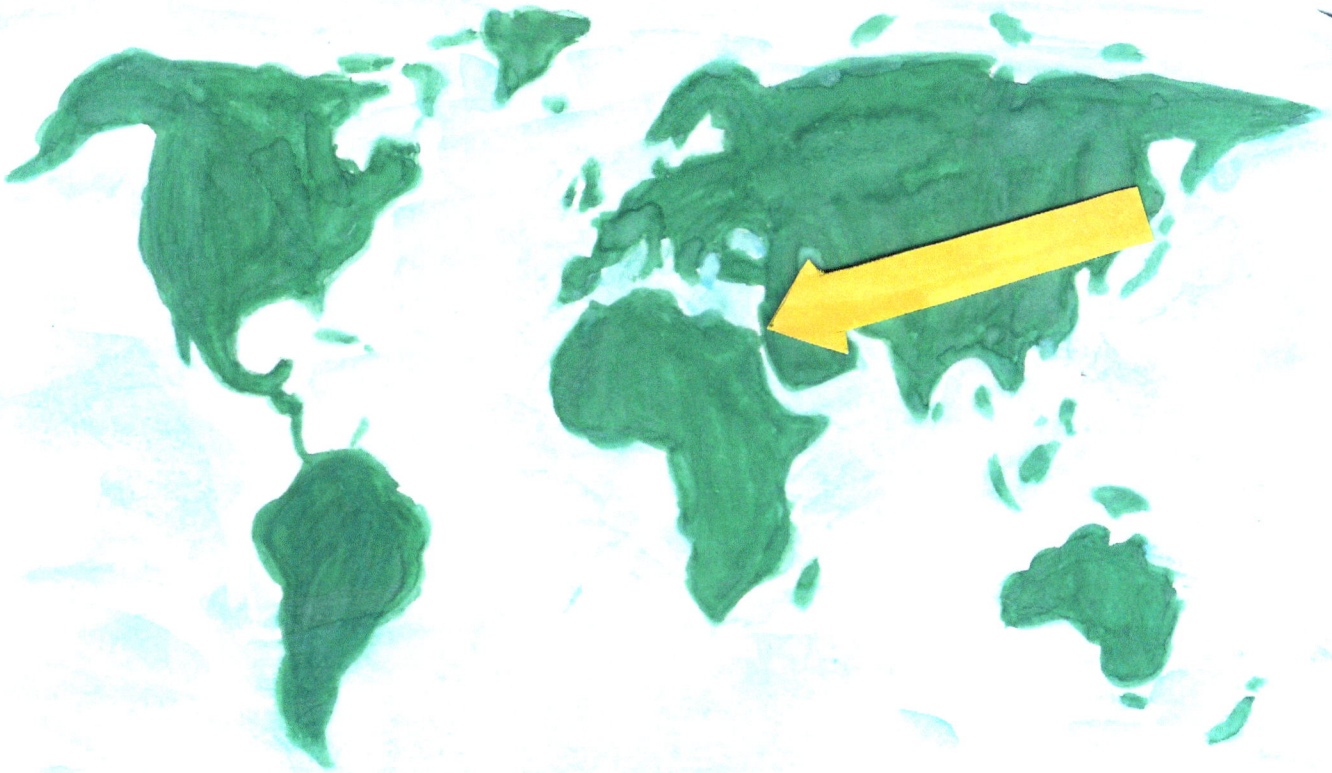

Jacob Lawrence was a Black American painter, professor and storyteller best known for showing what life was like for Black Americans through his art. He was born in 1917 in Atlantic City, New Jersey. His childhood was difficult; his parents divorced, and he spent several years in foster care. When he was 13, he and his siblings moved to Harlem in New York City, where they reconnected with their mother. Young Jacob copied patterns of his mother's carpets with crayons, and he found that he loved to create patterns of his own.

A few years later, he worked at a laundromat to make a living while attending art classes. Jacob Lawrence became one of the first artists trained by Black teachers during a time when creative culture in Harlem was thriving. In 1941 he married another painter, Gwendolyn Knight, and they enjoyed a lifelong relationship working together.

That year, he painted a 60-panel set of paintings now called *Migration Series*. The series portrayed the recent history of Black Americans moving from farm life in the South to Northern cities. *Migration Series* earned national recognition when it was displayed in New York at the Museum of Modern Art. He was the first Black artist to have his work featured there!

Later that same year, life changed for Americans when Japan attacked Pearl Harbor, drawing the United States into World War II. Jacob Lawrence served in the Coast Guard with the first racially integrated crew on his ship. When the war was over, he painted another famous series called *War Series* to tell stories of wartime through art. The Lawrences moved to Seattle, where he became an art professor at the University of Washington.

Jacob Lawrence taught his students, "My belief is that it is most important for an artist to develop an approach and philosophy about life - if he has developed this philosophy, he does not put paint on the canvas, he puts himself on canvas."

Putting himself on the canvas was something Jacob Lawrence did very well. His art is noted for bringing the Black American experience to life by using crisp shapes and bright colors against black and dark brown shades. Almost always, he painted people moving. His favorite scenes to paint were everyday life in Harlem, and historical events and people.

Today you can see his work in many museums nationwide. If you go to the Times Square subway station, you can see his last custom-made public work, a mosaic mural called *New York in Transit*.

Jacob Lawrence began his long, successful career in art by coloring what he saw around him with crayons! So, grab the supplies around you, draw what you like, and you can be like artistic Jacob Lawrence!

Jacob Riis was a Danish-American reporter and photographer who used his talent to help very poor people in New York City. He was born in Denmark in 1849 to a poor family with 15 children. Sadly, all but two of his brothers and sisters died as children. Back in those days, it was common for children to die from diseases and poor living conditions. As an adult, he became determined to help families living in poverty.

When he grew up, Jacob Riis immigrated to the United States to find work as a carpenter. He arrived in bustling New York City, where the population had boomed just a few years after the Civil War's end. There were pockets of many different immigrant nationalities living in one small space. This made the Lower East Side of New York the most densely populated place in the world!

The poor immigrants who lived there were packed into filthy, tiny apartments called tenements. It was common for 10 to 15 people to live in a single room. If one person had a disease, it would quickly spread to everyone living in the tenement. The wealthy didn't know about the living conditions of the poor and usually didn't care either.

Jacob Riis was underpaid as a carpenter and handyman, and he lived in the slums of New York City. He married Elisabeth Gjortz and then got a job as a police reporter working at the New York Tribune in the most crime-ridden slums of the city. Using his natural gift for writing, Jacob Riis wrote articles for the public about the slums with the goal of bringing about change.

Writing was helpful, but pictures of the disgusting tenements were what he really needed to make his point stronger. At that time, photography was a recent invention, and cameras didn't come with a flash feature to use in dark rooms. So, he tried drawing pictures of his experiences in the tenements, but his sketches didn't show the horrid living conditions well enough.

Then in 1887, Jacob Riis read about a new way to take pictures using a flash of light. This changed everything for his reporting! The first flash photography used chemical-filled powder in a pistol-like device that was dangerous. Later this progressed to a safer method of lighting the powder on a frying pan before taking the picture. Jacob Riis and his small team were the among first Americans to use flash photography. Because of this, he is considered one of the fathers of photography! Jacob Riis began to use his photographs to speak publicly about the filthy living conditions, urging people to help change them.

In 1889, Jacob Riis wrote a lengthy article, *How the Other Half Lives*, which included 19 of his photographs of the slums. The article became a book, which gained a lot of attention nationwide, as Jacob Riis had hoped. He wrote more books, including an autobiography where he emphasized his opinion that the United States is a land of great opportunity, even for poor immigrants like himself.

Future President Theodore Roosevelt introduced himself to Jacob Riis and offered to help him in any way he could. He got his chance when he became President of the Board of Commissioners of the New York City Police Department. Jacob Riis brought Theodore Roosevelt with him for his nighttime police work, and the laziness of many police officers was exposed. Theodore Roosevelt sprang into action, using his authority to correct the wrongdoings. Deeply moved by Jacob Riis' sense of justice, Theodore Roosevelt called him "the most useful citizen of New York" and "the best American I ever knew." The two became lifelong friends.

In 1891, Jacob Riis may well have saved New York City from a huge outbreak of a deadly disease called cholera. Suspecting that the city's drinking water was not clean, he took his camera to a watershed and snapped pictures of it. The drinking water had indeed been polluted by the sewage of nearby towns. Then, checking his findings with doctors, he wrote a column on the issue and ran it in the newspaper. New Yorkers were furious and demanded that the city leaders fix the problem. So, the leaders were forced to take action to clean the drinking water.

Jacob Riis urged city leaders to investigate unsafe tenements. He irritated some landlords when he campaigned to tear down the slums and replace them with a park. It took years, but finally he had success in his efforts. Thanks to Jacob Riis and others like him, people began to live longer, healthier lives.

It's easy to see what's wrong with the world and just complain about it. It's a lot harder take action to fix what is wrong. We learn from Jacob Riis to be a problem solver, not a complainer. When you face a problem, tackle it head on and you can be like unstoppable Jacob Riis!

Jacob Grimm was a German scholar and author best known for working with his brother to write and publish *Grimm's Fairy Tales*. He was born in 1785 in Germany, the oldest child in his family. He had a close friendship with his brother Wilhelm. Following in their father's footsteps, the brothers decided to study law and went to the University of Marburg together.

After they graduated, they got jobs in their field, but something else sparked their interest - local folklore. Storytelling used to be a popular tradition, but it was slowly dying. Over 100 years earlier, an invention made printing books a lot less expensive. After that, most people read more and told stories less. The Grimm brothers preserved their local heritage by talking with local townspeople and writing their stories. They published two volumes of books filled with these stories called *Children's and Household Tales*. Later this collection became known as *Grimm's Fairy Tales*.

Over the next few decades, *Grimm's Fairy Tales* was translated into dozens of languages and then handed down through the centuries. You probably recognize stories that they wrote like *Cinderella, Briar Rose* (also called *Sleeping Beauty), Snow White, Little Red Riding Hood, Rapunzel* and *Rumpelstiltskin*. These stories have been retold and adapted to be less scary for children today.

A lesser-known accomplishment of Jacob Grimm was his great contribution to the German language. He researched the history of the language and published *German Grammar*. He explained connections between grammatical rules in German and other European and Asian languages. So, his research works to explain languages in general.

Maybe you have brothers or sisters. Think about how much you can achieve if you work with them happily! If the Grimm brothers wrote most of the fairy tales we know, just think of what you and your siblings or friends might accomplish by working together!

Jacob Berzelius was a Swedish chemist who made contributions so great that he is called one of the founders of modern chemistry. He was born Jöns Jacob Berzelius in Ostergotland in 1779, and he always went by the name Jacob. When he was eight, he was orphaned and raised by relatives. As he grew, Jacob Berzelius developed a knack for science and medicine. He studied medicine and chemistry at Uppsala University.

Early on in his career, he was a physician. Then he became a professor in medicine and surgery in Stockholm. There, while writing a textbook, he made an important discovery about inorganic compounds. Based on this discovery, he created the table of atomic weights, which included every known element. To simplify his chart, Jacob Berzelius created a system of simple labels in Latin that we still use today. C represents carbon, Fe represents iron, and so forth. He used numbers to show the quantities of the elements, which we also still use today. So, for example, water is two hydrogens and one oxygen, or H_2O.

During his work as a chemist, Jacob Berzelius discovered four new elements, and his students discovered two more. His discoveries didn't end there! He was the first person to show the difference between organic compounds, which are made with carbon, and inorganic compounds, which are not made with carbon. While working with a friend, Jacob Berzelius created the word "protein," when they found that all proteins seemed to have the same formula. He was an eager teacher, and many great scientists after him built on his work.

His lab was always a mess, and he often said, "A tidy laboratory means a lazy chemist." Jacob Berzelius wasn't afraid to make mistakes and big messes in his discoveries. So don't be afraid to get messy and make mistakes when you are learning something new, and you can be like smart Jacob Berzelius!

Jacob Francis was a Black American Revolutionary war hero. He was born in 1754 in New Jersey. He worked for five different men by the time he turned 21, probably as an indentured servant. An indentured servant is someone who must work unpaid for an employer for a set time, usually to settle a debt. This system is illegal today since it is considered a form of slavery.

When Jacob Francis was freed, the Revolutionary War began between Britain and the United States. He bravely joined as a soldier in Massachusetts. At first, Black men were not allowed to join the Army, but months into the war, it was clear that more soldiers were needed. So free Black men were temporarily allowed to become soldiers. Although Jacob Francis faced discrimination, he proved to be a very skilled soldier. His unit helped the Americans reclaim Boston, and in New York they fought in the Battle of Long Island. They moved farther south to New Jersey, where General George Washington led the troops across the icy Delaware River in the two Battles of Trenton.

At the time, the United States Continental Army was seriously lacking resources, owing Jacob Francis and many other soldiers pay for their service. After 14 months of service, his time in the Army was over and Jacob Francis was honorably dismissed. He went back to his childhood home for the first time in many years to search for his mother, and he found her in poor health. Wanting to stay close to her, Jacob Francis did not return to his unit to receive the money owed to him, but instead joined the New Jersey militia. He served there until 1781, when the Americans won the war.

Jacob Francis was hard-working, which paid off when he purchased a house and many acres of land in New Jersey. This was a major accomplishment for a free Black man living under laws and attitudes that favored White people. A few years later, Jacob Francis married a slave named Mary, purchased her freedom, and together they had eight children. Decades later, in 1832, he finally requested the money owed to him by the United States government. In doing so, he provided for Mary, even after his death.

Jacob Francis was a great American patriot. The next time you see an American flag, give it a salute and think about Jacob Francis!

Jakob Dylan is an American singer and songwriter best known for two things: being the lead singer of a rock band called The Wallflowers and being the son of folk legend Bob Dylan.

He was born in 1969, the youngest of Bob and Sara Dylan's five children. They divorced when he was little, and he was raised by his mother in Los Angeles. Jakob Dylan always had a knack for music and art. He began playing guitars and writing songs when he was a teenager.

After graduating from high school, he and some friends formed a band called The Wallflowers. They had hits like "One Headlight" and "6th Avenue Heartache." He made some successful solo albums too. Like his father, Jakob Dylan has a gravelly voice which he combines with somewhat mysterious lyrics. Through all his success, Jakob Dylan realizes that he still lives in his father's shadow.

In an interview with the *New York Times*, he humbly stated, "Look, he's the best at what I do. I know that, and so do my heroes." Jakob Dylan also confessed that people always tell him that they love his dad's work. Jakob Dylan has opened for his father in concert, and the two of them have a great relationship, although neither of them like to talk about it publicly too much.

A family man, Jakob Dylan and his wife, Paige, have four sons together. He was given a Father of the Year award from the American Diabetes Association in 2014. The award recognizes men that have made family, career and community a priority. The American Diabetes Association is one of many great organizations that Jakob Dylan regularly supports with his talent and money.

If you ever feel like you have big shoes to fill, do your own thing, and keep singing your song like talented Jakob Dylan!

Jacob Bronowski was a Polish-born British mathematician who developed a human-centered approach to science. He was born in 1908 in Poland, and as a boy he moved to Germany, then to Britain. He studied mathematics at the University of Cambridge and graduated with a Ph.D. at the top of his class.

Jacob Bronowski married Rita Coblentz in 1941, and together they had four children. When they married, World War II had begun, and he served in the British military. His job was to make bombing the enemy more effective. The war ended in 1945 when the United States dropped atomic bombs on two Japanese cities. Afterward, Jacob Bronowski went with a team of scientists to those cities to study the harmful effects of the atomic bombs. Using his research there, he predicted the terrible long-term effects of nuclear warfare. When he went back to Britain, things were never the same for him again. Jacob Bronowski had a whole new mission.

He wrote several books and spoke on the radio about his new belief that science needed to be morally good to in order to work. In other words, science should make everyone's life better, not worse. These books shaped people's views during the Cold War, a time when the Soviet Union and the United States built up nuclear weapons so powerful that they could have destroyed the entire world. Thankfully, world leaders listened to Jacob Bronowski and people like him to save the world from destruction.

It's always a good idea to ask yourself whether the decisions that you are making are morally good. Whatever you decide to do in life, use your abilities to be helpful, not harmful, and you can be like empathetic Jacob Bronowski!

This page is all about you!

_____ was born on

_____

As a baby, Jacob _____

_____

As a little boy, Jacob _____

_____

Jacob is especially good at _____

_____

Jacob is often described as _____

_____

Jacob makes people laugh when he _____

_____

One day Jacob would like to _____

_____

This page is for making a self-portrait. A self-portrait is a picture of you, drawn by you!

Bibliography

Biography.com Editors. "Jacob Grimm Biography." *The Biography.com website.* A&E Television Networks. 02 Apr. 2014. Web. 14 Mar. 2019

Decurtis, Anthony. "Dylan breaks silence on 'my dad.'" *nytimes.com* The New York Times, 10 May 2005. Web. 20 Mar. 2019.

Encyclopaedia Britannica Editors. "Jacob Bronowski." *Encyclopaedia Britannica.* Encyclopaedia Britannica, inc. 14 Jan. 2019. Web. 15 Mar. 2019.

Encyclopaedia Britannica Editors. "Jacob Riis." *Encyclopaedia Britannica.* Encyclopaedia Britannica, inc. 07 Feb. 2019. Web. 21 Feb. 2019.

Kidder, Larry. "The American Revolution of Private Jacob Francis." *allthingsliberty.com.* Journal of the American Revolution, Web. 20 Mar. 2019

Melhado, Evan. "Jons Jacob Berzelius." *Encyclopaedia Britannica.* Encyclopaedia Britannica, inc. 26 Feb. 2019. Web. 18 Mar. 2019.

Robinson, Karina. "Jacob Francis (1754-1836)." *BlackPast.org.* BlackPast Remembered & Reclaimed, 26 Jul. 2013. Web. 20 Mar. 2019

Wikipedia contributors. "Jacob (name)." *Wikipedia, The Free Encyclopedia.* Wikipedia, The Free Encyclopedia, 17 Jan. 2019. Web. 14 Feb. 2019.

Wikipedia contributors. "Jöns Jacob Berzelius." *Wikipedia, The Free Encyclopedia*. Wikipedia, The Free Encyclopedia, 23 Feb. 2019. Web. 18 Mar. 2019.

Wikipedia contributors. "Jacob Bronowski." *Wikipedia, The Free Encyclopedia*. Wikipedia, The Free Encyclopedia, 19 Feb. 2019. Web. 15 Mar. 2019.

Wikipedia contributors. "Jakob Dylan." *Wikipedia, The Free Encyclopedia*. Wikipedia, The Free Encyclopedia, 8 Mar. 2019. Web. 20 Mar. 2019.

Wikipedia contributors. "Jacob Grimm." *Wikipedia, The Free Encyclopedia*. Wikipedia, The Free Encyclopedia, 6 Mar. 2019. Web. 14 Mar. 2019.

Wikipedia contributors. "Jacob Lawrence." *Wikipedia, The Free Encyclopedia*. Wikipedia, The Free Encyclopedia, 4 Mar. 2019. Web. 8 Mar. 2019.

Wikipedia contributors. "Jacob Riis." *Wikipedia, The Free Encyclopedia*. Wikipedia, The Free Encyclopedia, 7 Dec. 2018. Web. 22 Feb. 2019.

www.ingramcontent.com/pod-product-compliance
Lightning Source LLC
Chambersburg PA
CBHW042111040426
42448CB00002B/223